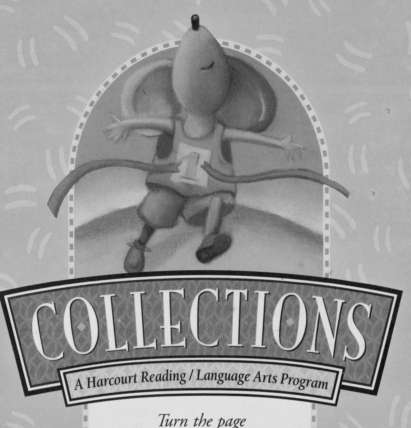

COLLECTIONS

A Harcourt Reading / Language Arts Program

*Turn the page
and say hello
to new friends.*

COLLECTIONS

A Harcourt Reading / Language Arts Program

JOIN IN

SENIOR AUTHORS

Roger C. Farr • Dorothy S. Strickland

AUTHORS

Richard F. Abrahamson • Alma Flor Ada • Bernice E. Cullinan • Margaret McKeown • Nancy Roser
Patricia Smith • Judy Wallis • Junko Yokota • Hallie Kay Yopp

SENIOR CONSULTANT

Asa G. Hilliard III

CONSULTANTS

Karen S. Kupiter • David A. Monti • Angelina Olivares

Harcourt

Orlando   Boston   Dallas   Chicago   San Diego

Visit *The Learning Site!*
www.harcourtschool.com

Dear Reader,

Join In and meet some new friends! Visit an ant's surprise birthday party. See what happens when six little fish meet six little feet. Find out where frogs really come from. Then find out what's inside Daniel's mystery egg. Turn the page and say hello!

Sincerely,

The Authors

The Authors

THEME

It's My Turn Now

4

CONTENTS

It's My Turn Now

6

Reader's Choice

Sid and Sam

by Nola Buck

Two friends start singing together. One friend just can't stop singing!

Award-Winning Illustrator

FROM THE LIBRARY

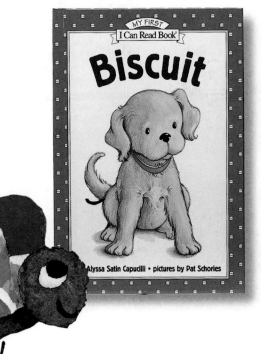

Biscuit
by Alyssa Satin Capucilli

Biscuit finds that he needs a little help getting ready for bed.

Award-Winning Illustrator

FROM THE LIBRARY

I Am Six
by Ann Morris

Children enjoy a day at their school.

Award-Winning Author

READER'S CHOICE BOOK

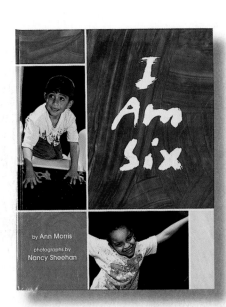

by Patti Trimble
illustrated by Daniel Moreton

WHAT DAY IS IT?

WHAT
DAY
IS IT?

written by Patti Trimble
illustrated by Daniel Moreton

Gil was glad.
"This is my big day!"

Gil saw Ann.
"Ann! What day is it?"

"It's Monday," said Ann.

Gil was sad.
"Ann forgot my big day."

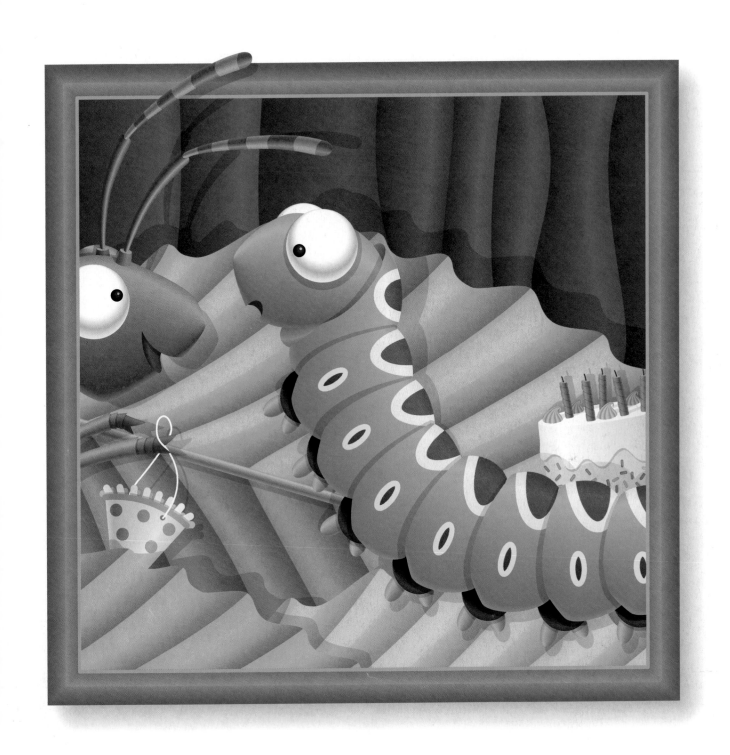

Gil saw Todd.
"Todd! What day is it?"

"It's Monday," said Todd.

"Ann and Todd forgot that
this is my big day!"

Gil was so sad.
"My friends forgot."

"It's my birthday, and
they missed it."

"We did not miss it!
Happy Birthday, Gil!"

"Thank you," said Gil.
"This is a surprise!"

Meet the Illustrator

Daniel Moreton

As a child, Daniel Moreton loved listening to his grandmother's stories. They made him want to write his own. Daniel Moreton loves to make pictures for stories, too. He uses a computer to draw them.

ANT
BOOKMARK

Gil's friends remembered his birthday. Make a bookmark to help you remember your place.

1 Draw an ant at the top of your bookmark.

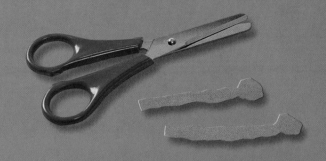

2 Cut out two antennas.

3 Glue them on the ant's head.

Gil is a funny ant.

4 Write a sentence about Gil the ant.

Share your bookmark with a classmate.

Moving Day

written by Anthony G. Brandon

illustrated by Wong Herbert Yee

It was moving day.
Mr. and Mrs. Kim were moving.

Jenny Kim was moving.
Jack Kim was moving.

28

But not Annie.

"I'm not going," said Annie.
She sat on a box.

"Let's go," said Mrs. Kim.
"I'm not going," said Annie.

"You have to go," said Jenny.
"I'm not going," said Annie.

"We all have to go," said Jack.
"Well, I'm not going," said Annie.

"You will have a big yard,"
said Mrs. Kim.

"I like my little yard better!"
said Annie.

"You will have a big room,"
said Mr. Kim.

"I like my little room better!"
said Annie.

"You will make new friends,"
said Jenny.

"I like my old friends better,"
said Annie.

It was time to go.

"Annie, get the last box," said Mrs. Kim.
"OK, but I'm still not going," said Annie.

"Is this puppy going?"

"Yes," they all said.

"Then I'm going, too!" said Annie.

Wong Herbert Yee

Where do you get ideas for your stories?

I think about everything around me. I think about myself as a little boy and about my daughter when she was a first grader.

What is your favorite thing to draw?

I like drawing animals—especially animals wearing clothes! The rabbit in "Moving Day" is special to me because it is my daughter's favorite stuffed animal. I like to put this rabbit in every story I do.

Wong Herbert Yee

46

Homes On

These homes are easy to move. Can you see why? Some people live in homes like these. Why might they want homes that are easy to move?

American Indian tepees

the Move

Central Asian yurts

Tent

RESPONSE ACTIVITY

Pack Your Suitcase

Pretend it is your moving day. What special things will you pack? Make a suitcase for your things.

You will need:

construction paper

pipe cleaners

crayons

magazines

scissors

glue

hole punch

1. Fold the paper in half.

2. Make a handle for each side.

3. Fill your suitcase with pictures.

Ask a friend to guess what is in your suitcase. Then **show** and **tell** what you have.

How Many Fish?

by Caron Lee Cohen
illustrated by S.D. Schindler

How many fish?
How many fish?

Six little fish in the bay.

Where do they go?
Why do they go?

Six little fish on their way.

How many feet?
How many feet?

Six little feet in the bay.

Where do they go?
Why do they go?

60

Six little feet on their way.

How many fish?

How many fish?

One yellow fish in the bay.

Where's yellow fish?
Where's yellow fish?

64

Poor yellow fish lost its way.

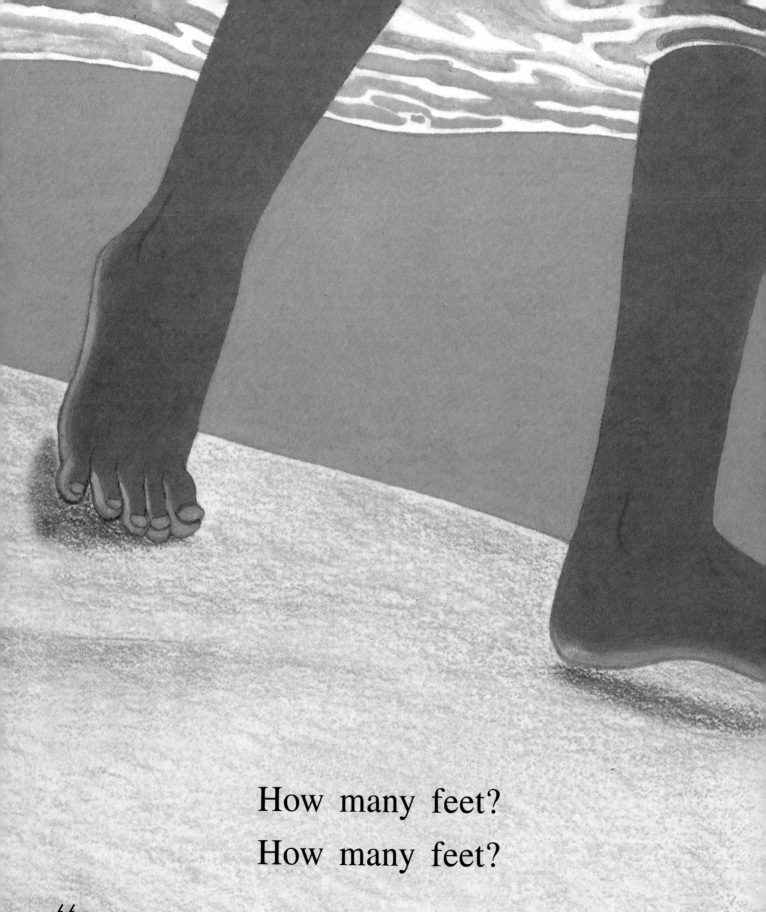

How many feet?

How many feet?

Two little feet in the bay.

Where's the red pail?
Where's the red pail?

Two little feet dash away.

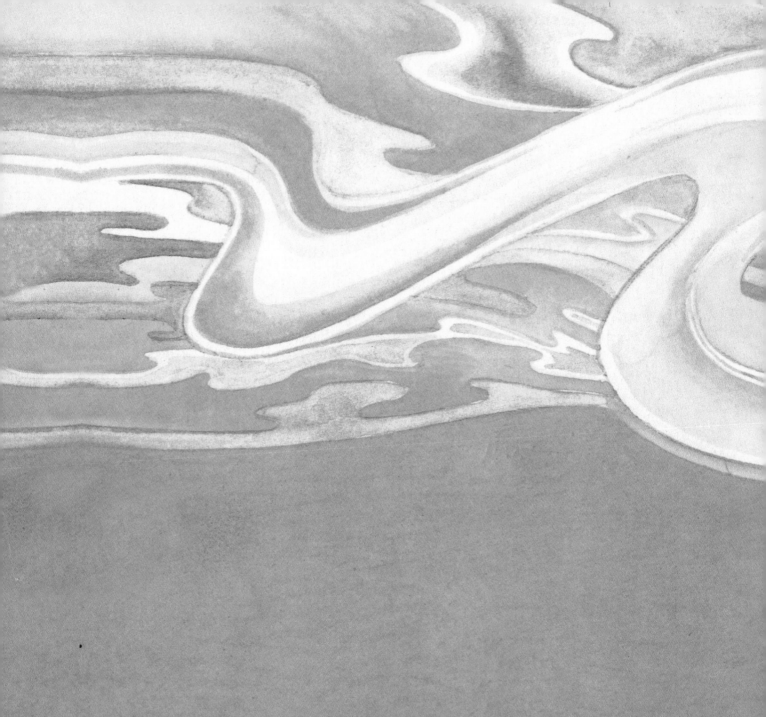

One happy fish.
One happy fish.

One happy fish on its way!

How many fish?
How many fish?

Six little fish in the bay!

Meet the Author

Caron Lee Cohen

Caron Lee Cohen enjoys spending
summers at the beach. She loves to
swim in the ocean, where she has been
eye-to-eye with many fish! She wrote
How Many Fish? to share the fun. Caron
Lee Cohen hopes that you will meet fish
someday, too.

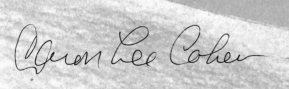

Meet the Illustrator
S.D. Schindler

S.D. Schindler was the best artist in his class when he was growing up. All the other children loved his drawings. Now he draws pictures for many books.

S.D. Schindler likes fish a lot. He made two small ponds near his house for goldfish. He loves to sit and watch them swim!

Fantastic Fish

Fish live in water. They have special body parts called gills that help them breathe.

Some kinds of fish swim together in large groups called schools. A fish may stay in the same school its whole life!

Lion fish

Butterfly fish

Fish have many shapes and sizes. Some fish are very strange-looking.

Sea horse

Starfish

Jelly fish

Stingray

There are many kinds of sea animals. Each kind has its own way of living in the waters of the sea.

Fish Finders

Play a game called Fish Finder with a partner!

1. Work with a partner and make six fish.

2. Lay them in a row.

3. Take turns being the fish hider and the fish finder. The fish finder must not look.

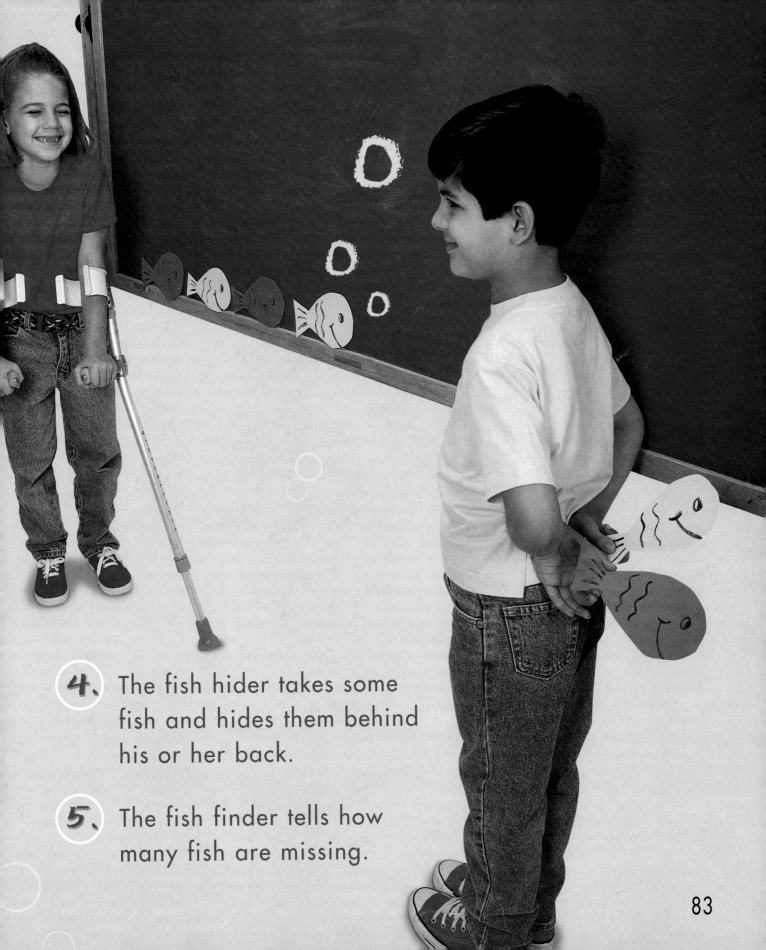

4. The fish hider takes some fish and hides them behind his or her back.

5. The fish finder tells how many fish are missing.

83

Kit and Kat

Award-Winning Illustrator

by
Tomie dePaola

KIT and KAT

Written and
illustrated by
Tomie dePaola

Kit's Pajamas

Today was a big day for Kit and Kat.

They were going to sleep at
Grandma and Grandpa's house.

Kit and Kat got out their stuff.

Soon they were ready.

"Do you have everything?"
asked Grandma.
"Yes," said Kit.
"Yes," said Kat.

So off they went.

Kit and Kat had fun.

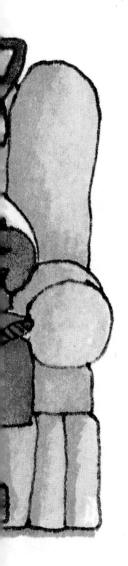

Grandpa gave the best rides.
Grandma read the best stories.

Soon it was time for bed.

Kat put on her pajamas.
But Kit could not find his.

"I left them at home!" said Kit.
And he began to cry.

"Don't cry," said Grandpa. "Look!"
"Oh, Grandpa," said Kit.
"Your pajama top!"

"You look like a little Grandpa,"
said Kat.

Then they both went to sleep.

Meet the Author/Illustrator
Tomie dePaola

Tomie dePaola had a playful kitten named Rosalie. He had an old cat named Satie, too. He loved to watch the two cats play. He said that Rosalie acted just like a child. So Tomie drew Kit and Kat to look like Rosalie. He drew Grandma and Grandpa to look like Satie.

100

New Clothes for Kit

Kit looks funny in Grandpa's pajama top.

How would Kit look in some other clothes?

1. Draw Kit's face on a card.

2. Draw Kit's feet on a card.

3. Draw some clothes for Kit.

102

4. Try on Kit's new clothes! Which outfit does Kit like the best?

5. Trade outfits with a classmate. Make up things Kit might say about his new clothes.

103

Where Do Frogs Come From?

by Alex Vern

Frogs come from eggs. These black dots are frog eggs.

Pop!
Tadpoles pop out
of the eggs.

The tadpoles swim fast
to get away from fish.
Fish eat tadpoles!

At first, a tadpole
doesn't look like a frog.
It has a long tail.

Tadpoles eat plants.
They eat a lot
and grow fast.

Soon, strong back legs
form. They help the tadpole
kick as it swims.

Small front legs
form, too. The tadpole
still has a tail.

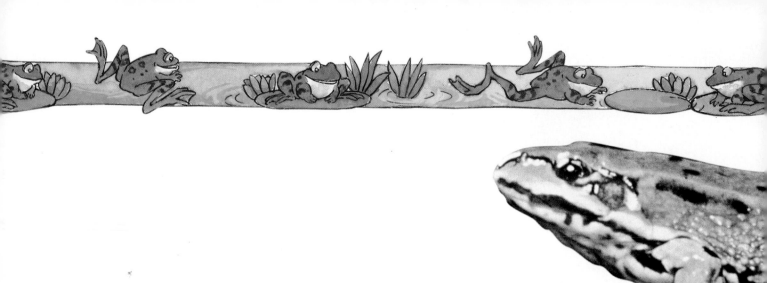

Now the tadpole's
tail is gone. At last
it's a big, strong frog.

112

Hop!
The frog pushes off.

Frogs eat lots of bugs.
Mmmm, good!

From Egg to Frog

1. Egg

2. Tadpole

3. Frog

Polliwogs

by Kristine O'Connell George
illustrated by Jui Ishida

Come see
What I found!
Chubby commas,
Mouths round,
Plump babies,
Stubby as toes.
Polliwogs!
Tadpoles!

Come see
What I found!
Frogs-in-waiting—
Huddled in puddles,
Snuggled in mud.

117

FROG  CHAIN

Make a paper chain that shows how tadpoles become frogs.

118

1 Think about how tadpoles change.

2 Draw five changes on paper strips.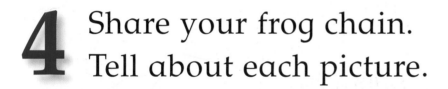

3 Make the paper strips into a chain.

4 Share your frog chain. Tell about each picture.

Daniel's Mystery Egg

by Alma Flor Ada

Illustrated by G. Brian Karas

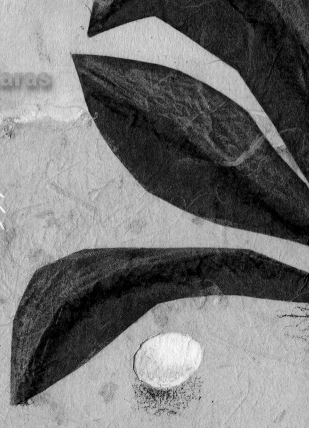

Daniel's
Mystery
Egg

by Alma Flor Ada
Illustrated by G. Brian Karas

Award-Winning
Author and
Illustrator

120

Daniel found a surprise.
It was a small, white egg.
He put it in a little box.

Daniel ran to tell Alex. "Look! This is the best egg ever! What could it be?"

"Maybe it will be an ostrich with a long neck!"said Alex.

"You can take it to school for show-and-tell.
I can help you."

"I won't need help," said Daniel. "I think
a small animal will come out of this egg."

Next, Meg came to look. "Daniel found this egg," said Alex. "What could it be?"

"Maybe it will be an alligator with big teeth!" said Meg.

"Alligators are not good pets. Maybe you will have to move out of your house. You can all move in with me!"

"We won't need to move," said Daniel.
"I think a nice animal will come out of
this egg."

Next, Tammy came to look. "Daniel found an egg!" said Meg. "What could it be?"

"Maybe it will be a duck
that quacks all the time!"
said Tammy.

"Your house will be very noisy. You will have to teach the duck to quack softly. I can help you."

"I don't think the house will be noisy," said Daniel. "I think a quiet animal will come out of this egg."

"Well, Daniel," said Alex, "What will
this small, nice, quiet animal be?"
"We'll have to wait and see," said Daniel.

So they waited,
and waited,
and waited . . .

136

Then one day the egg hatched!

"It doesn't have a long neck," said Alex.
"It doesn't have big teeth," said Meg.
"It doesn't have a noisy quack," said Tammy.

"No," said Daniel. "But it IS small, nice, and quiet. It's the best lizard ever!"

Meet the Author
Alma Flor Ada

Alma Flor Ada learned to read out in the
garden. Her grandmother taught her by
writing the names of plants in the dirt. Even
now, Alma Flor Ada's favorite place to read
and write is outdoors. Many of her stories
are about animals and nature.

Alma Flor Ada

140

Meet the Illustrator
Brian Karas

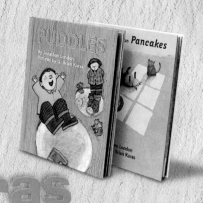

Brian Karas used to live in Arizona. There he saw lots of lizards like Daniel's.

Brian Karas made pictures for this story in an interesting way. First he glued bits of different kinds of paper on white paper. Then he painted pictures on this background.

"Sometimes I tear up my old artwork," he says, "and use it in my collages. I hope you'll try making and painting collages, too. It's fun!"

Brian Karas

Guess the Animal!

You have met Daniel's lizard. Write a riddle about another animal.

1. Think of an animal.

2. Write three clues about it.

3. Trade clues with a classmate.

4. Read the clues.

It is green.

It eats bugs.

It is smaller than a book.

Try to guess the animal.

143

Acknowledgments

For permission to reprint copyrighted material, grateful acknowledgment is made to the following sources:

Bantam Books, a division of Random House, Inc.: Cover illustration by S. D. Schindler from *Eency Weency Spider* by Joanne Oppenheim. Illustration copyright ©1991 by S. D. Schindler and Byron Preiss Visual Publications, Inc.

Clarion Books/Houghton Mifflin Company: "Polliwogs" from *The Great Frog Race and Other Poems* by Kristine O'Connell George. Text copyright ©1997 by Kristine O'Connell George.

Greenwillow Books, a division of William Morrow & Company, Inc.: Cover illustration by Nancy Barnet from *Where's the Fly?* by Caron Lee Cohen. Illustration copyright ©1996 by Nancy Barnet. Cover illustration by Peter Sis from *Three Yellow Dogs* by Caron Lee Cohen. Illustration copyright ©1986 by Peter Sis.

Grosset & Dunlap, a division of Penguin Putnam Inc.: "Kit's Pajamas" from *Kit and Kat* by Tomie dePaola. Copyright ©1986 by The Phillip Lief Group; new material copyright ©1994 by Grosset & Dunlap, Inc.

Harcourt, Inc.: Cover illustration from *Pancakes for Breakfast* by Tomie dePaola. Copyright ©1978 by Tomie dePaola.

HarperCollinsChildren'sBooks, a division of HarperCollins Publishers, Inc.: Cover illustration by G. Brian Karas from *Sid and Sam* by Nola Buck. Illustration copyright ©1996 by G. Brian Karas. Cover illustration by Pat Schories from *Biscuit* by Alyssa Satin Capucilli. Illustration copyright ©1996 by Pat Schories. From *How Many Fish?* by Caron Lee Cohen, illustrated by S. D. Schindler. Text copyright ©1998 by Caron Lee Cohen; illustrations copyright ©1998 by S. D. Schindler.

Houghton Mifflin Company: Cover illustration from *Mrs. Brown Went to Town* by Wong Herbert Yee. Copyright ©1996 by Wong Herbert Yee. Cover illustration from *EEK! There's a Mouse in the House* by Wong Herbert Yee. Copyright ©1992 by Wong Herbert Yee. Cover illustration from *Fireman Small* by Wong Herbert Yee. Copyright ©1994 by Wong Herbert Yee. Cover illustration from *Big Black Bear* by Wong Herbert Yee. Copyright ©1993 by Wong Herbert Yee.

Laredo Publishing Company, Inc.: Cover illustration by Vivi Escrivá from *Olmo and the Blue Butterfly* by Alma Flor Ada. Copyright ©1993 by Laredo Publishing Co., Inc.

Penguin Putnam Books for Young Readers, a division of Penguin Putnam Inc.: Cover illustration by Tomie dePaola from *Mice Squeak, We Speak* by Arnold L. Shapiro. Illustration copyright ©1997 by Tomie dePaola.

Santillana USA Publishing Company, Inc.: Cover illustration by Vivi Escrivá from *The Empty Piñata* by Alma Flor Ada. Copyright ©1993 by Santillana Publishing Co., Inc.

Silver Burdett Press, a division of Modern Curriculum, Inc., Simon & Schuster Education Group: Cover photographs by Nancy Sheehan from *I Am Six* by Ann Morris. Photographs copyright ©1995 by Nancy Sheehan.

Simon & Schuster Books for Young Readers, an imprint of Simon & Schuster

Children's Publishing Division: Cover illustration by S. D. Schindler from *Those Amazing Ants* by Patricia Brennan Demuth. Illustration copyright ©1994 by S. D. Schindler. Cover illustration from *Charlie Needs a Cloak* by Tomie dePaola. Copyright ©1973 by Tomie dePaola.

Stewart, Tabori and Chang, Publishers: Cover illustration from *Martí and the Mango* by Daniel Moreton. Copyright ©1993 by Daniel Moreton.

Turtle Books: Cover illustration from *La Cucaracha Martina* by Daniel Moreton. Copyright ©1997 by Daniel Moreton.

Photo Credits

Key: (T)=top, (B)=bottom, (C)=center, (L)=left, (R)=right
Page 23, Walt Chyrnwski / Black Star; 24, 25, Campos Photography; 47, Santa Fabio / Black Star; 48-49, Bachmann / Photo Researchers; 48 (inset), Lawrence Migdale; 49(t), Ken Cole / Earth Scenes; 49(b), Francois Gohier / Photo Researchers; 76, Walt Chyrnwski / Black Star; 77, Sal DiMarco; 78, Photodisc; 79, David Hall / Photo Researchers; 80(butterfly fish), Stephen Frink / Tony Stone Images; (starfish), Darryl Torckler / Tony Stone Images; (seahorse), Kjell Sandved / Visuals Unlimited; (frog), A. Flowers & L. Newman / Photo Researchers; (lionfish), David Hall / Photo Researchers; 81(t), Mark Harmel / Tony Stone Images; 81(c), Marc Chamberlain / Tony Stone Image; 81(b), Stephen Frink / Tony Stone Images; 83, Ken Kinzie / Harcourt; 101, Suki Coughlin; 103, Doug Dukane / Harcourt; 104-105, Joyce Photographics / Photo Researchers; 105, Hans Pfletschinger / Peter Arnold, Inc.; 106, K. Atkinson / OSF / Animals Animals; 107, William H. Mullins / Photo Researchers; 108, Gary Meszaros / Dembinsky Photo Associates; 109, Sharon Cummings / Dembinsky Photo Associates 110-111, C. Allan Morgan / Peter Arnold, Inc.; 111, Gary Meszaros / Dembinsky Photo Associates; 112-113, Stephen Dalton / Photo Researchers; 114(l), E.R. Degginger / Animals Animals; 114(r), Stephen Dalton / Animals Animals; 115(t), Hans Pfletschinger / Peter Arnold, Inc.; 115(c), Hans Pfletschinger / Peter Arnold, Inc. 115(b), Joe McDonald / DRK Photo; 118, 119, Campos Photography; 140(l), G. Brian Karas; 140(r), Dale Higgins.

Illustration Credits

Margaret Spengler, Cover Art; Michael Grejniec, 4-9; Daniel Moreton, 10-25; Wong Herbert Yee, 26-47; S.D. Schindle, 52-77; Tomie dePaola, 84-101; Doug Cushman, 108-109, 112-113; Jui Ishida, 116-117; Tracy Sabin, 118-119, 142-143; G. Brian Karas, 120-141